I've Got an IDEA!

THE STORY OF FREDERICK McKINLEY JONES

I've Got an IDEA!

Gloria M. Swanson
Margaret V. Ott

RP

Runestone Press • Minneapolis

12.94 – BT – 7.50
cop. 1

To our grandchildren,
Alex and Shannon;
Jami, Megan, Roy, Tammy, Richard, and Jessica

Our thanks to the people of Hallock who knew Fred in his younger years; to the people of Thermo King who knew him as a mechanical genius; to Lucille who shared his personal life, and to editor Marybeth Lorbiecki, who guided the authors in their telling of the story of Fred Jones.

RUNESTONE PRESS • ᚱᚢᚾᛏᚼᛏᛩᛏ

rune (r̄oon) *n* **1 a** : one of the earliest written alphabets used in northern Europe, dating back to A.D. 200; **b** : an alphabet character believed to have magic powers; **c** : a charm; **d** : an Old Norse or Finnish poem. **2** : a poem or incantation of mysterious significance, often carved in stone.

This book is available in two editions:
Library binding by Runestone Press
Soft cover by First Avenue Editions
Runestone Press and First Avenue Editions
℅ The Lerner Group
241 First Avenue North
Minneapolis, MN 55401

Library of Congress Cataloging-in-Publication Data
Swanson, Gloria Borseth.
    I've got an idea! : the story of Frederick McKinley Jones / by Gloria M.
Swanson & Margaret V. Ott.
       p.   cm.
    Includes bibliographical references (p. 91) and index.
    Summary: A biography of the black engineer and inventor credited with many inventions, including refrigeration units for trucks and railroad cars, portable X-ray units, and the ticket dispenser.
    ISBN 0-8225-3174-7 (lib. bdg.); ISBN 0-8225-9662-8 (pbk.)
    1. Jones, Frederick McKinley, 1893–1961—Juvenile literature. 2. Afro-American inventors—United States—Biography—Juvenile literature. [1. Jones, Frederick McKinley, 1893–1961.
2. Inventors. 3. Afro-Americans—Biography.] I. Ott, Virginia. II. Title.
T40.J59S93 1994
609.2—dc20
[B]
                93–7823
                CIP
                AC

Manufactured in the United States of America
1 2 3 4 5 6 – I/JR – 99 98 97 96 95 94

Contents

Left Behind

Five-year-old Fred Jones stared at his father's pocket watch, turned it over in his hand, and held it to his ear. Why did it tick? Fred sat down on the porch step and carefully pried open the back. He was fascinated by the tiny cogwheels turning next to each other. He saw the little spring near the stem his father wound every night before he went to bed. Fred would have to lift out some of the wheels to see what was underneath it.

When his father, John, came home from work, he found his son with pieces of the watch scattered around him. John just shook his head, smiled, and sat down on the end of the step. This was certainly not the first time. Time and again, John had found Fred tinkering with odd tools and abandoned gadgets. Watching his son take something apart to see how it worked and then put it back together was simply a wonderment to John. He didn't scold the boy. Fred never remembered his father ever punishing him.

This inquisitive child, Frederick McKinley Jones, was born on May 17, 1893, in Covington, Kentucky, on the south bank of the Ohio River. The Ohio River was the natural boundary between what were traditionally known as the Northern states and the Southern states.

Fred's father was a red-haired, blue-eyed Irishman who worked for the railroads. Fred's mother was an African American. In the 1800s, there were very few interracial marriages anywhere in the United States, and they were especially rare in the South. In most Southern states, inter- racial marriages were illegal. There were "Jim Crow" laws to keep blacks and whites separate in public and private places. There were separate schools, churches, hospitals, res- taurants, halls, and theaters for "coloreds" and for "whites." Those for whites were finer, cleaner, and more expensive. African Americans were forced to sit in the backs of trains or streetcars. They had to use their own separate drinking fountains and public restrooms.

An example of the separation between European Ameri- cans and African Americans enforced by Jim Crow laws

A view from the front of a bus in the Southern states in the early 1900s

Even where there weren't Jim Crow laws and interracial marriages *were* legal, they were not common. People, both white and black, often treated such couples and their children with prejudice and hatred. Fred's parents probably were not married. Fred never knew. He believed his mother died when he was young since his only early memories were of living with his father.

During these early years, John and Fred moved from rooming house to rooming house in whatever place there was work on the railroad tracks. John would pay the landladies to look after Fred while he was at work. Usually the boy was left to do as he pleased.

The older boys in the neighborhood often taunted Fred about being part black and part white. Fred remembered his father telling him many times not to pay a mind to what others said or the way they looked at him. John himself knew what it was like to be ridiculed.

Few Irish Americans had not endured insults and jeers. Thousands of Irish had come to the United States in the 1850s because there were no jobs and little food in Ireland. They were looked down upon in America. The only jobs they could find were the low-paying, hard labor jobs other Americans didn't want. Like Fred's father, many Irishmen went to work on the railroads that were being built all across the United States. For shelter, the men often put up shacks, which they had to abandon as they moved on down the tracks. John wanted a better home than this for his son. So he chose to live in rooming houses where someone could care for Fred while he was at work.

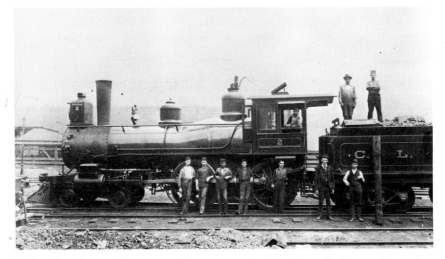

Railroad workers in Cincinnati, Ohio, across the river from Covington, Kentucky, near the turn of the century

When Fred was very small, his father made him a little wagon, using four discarded wheels. It rattled and wobbled along behind the small boy as he wandered down the street. So for Fred's sixth birthday, his father bought him a brand new wagon. Fred ran up and down the street pulling his toy. The new one was so much easier to pull!

All at once, Fred stopped short beside the old wagon.

Grabbing some tools, he began taking apart a wheel of the new wagon. Soon he held in his hand the two ball bearings. The small metal balls, like marbles, rolled freely in the channel near the center of the wheel, where it attached to the axle. Now he could see why the wheels of the new wagon could turn so smoothly—because nothing rubbed together. There were no ball bearings in the old wagon's wheels.

By the time Fred was seven, he was strong, independent, and big for his age. John would soon have to leave the area to find another place where railroad tracks needed repair. He knew that for his son's own good, Fred needed to stay in one place to attend school. He also knew that his son would have a better chance for an education in a Northern state, where there was less segregation.

One morning, Fred's father put his son's belongings in a box, and the two of them walked away from Covington, Kentucky, crossing the bridge over the Ohio River into Cincinnati, Ohio. They walked and walked until they came to the rectory of a Catholic church. John asked Fred to sit on the back step while he talked to the priest. When the men finished talking and came outside, Fred stood and looked up at his father. John slowly pulled out his watch. He laid it in his son's hand, rumpled his brown wavy hair, and said, "Be a good boy, son. I'll be back to get you when I can." Then he hurried away.

Fred never saw his father again. As long as he lived, tears would come to his eyes when he talked of the day his father left him.

That fall, the priest, Father Ryan, enrolled Fred in school. He was the tallest boy in the first grade. His desk was in the back row, where it was easy to daydream.

To earn his keep, Fred kept the grass mowed and the snow

shoveled. He learned to split firewood and scrub floors. He was taught to cook, bake biscuits, and get the meals started. Fred often quoted Father Ryan, "If you want to eat, you work!" Fred would even have to rise early to awaken Father Ryan and help him get dressed for mass.

It wasn't easy for Fred to live under the strict discipline of Father Ryan. School and work bored him. But Fred had nowhere else to go. He did what was expected of him, and he looked ahead to Saturdays, when the priest allowed Fred to do as he pleased.

After school, Fred frequently walked down the alleys on his way back to the rectory. He often passed Oscar, who would be polishing a big car. Oscar was an African American who worked as a chauffeur for a wealthy family. Part of his job was to keep the family's two large cars running and looking like new. A kind and patient man, Oscar knew how Fred worshiped these newfangled horseless carriages, so he saved the polishing and shining for Saturdays, when Fred was free to help him.

One Saturday morning when Fred was ten years old, Oscar had to take the sedan to Crothers' Garage in town for repairs, and he took Fred along for the ride. Once Fred walked into the garage, he never wanted to leave. Here, in one place, was everything he had dreamed of seeing—cars, engines, motors, and tools. Fred left with Oscar, but from that day on, he thought only of getting back to that garage.

Fred's desire to learn about machines became an obsession. Nothing else mattered. After living in the rectory for four years, twelve-year-old Fred ran away from Father Ryan, the school, and childhood. Still wearing knickers, Fred decided to make it on his own. R. C. Crothers' Garage was his first stop.

On His Own

Fred begged Mr. Crothers for a job, claiming he was fourteen and had been to high school. The boy looked older than his years, and Mr. Crothers needed someone to keep the garage swept. That was a Friday. He hired Fred to start work the following Monday. Fred, however, couldn't wait! At six o'clock the next morning, he was sitting outside Crothers' Garage waiting for the mechanics to show up.

Fred's job was to sweep the floors, to haul out rubbish, and to keep tools picked up and in order. This job was perfect for Fred. It gave him the freedom to roam the garage and watch the mechanics at work. He began to find answers to the questions that spilled over in his mind.

Gradually Fred eased himself into repair jobs. If a tire had to be changed, he would have it off before the mechanic got to it. Fred was the first at the garage each morning and the last to leave each night. The "eatin' money" he earned at the garage usually wasn't spent on food, but on car magazines. He couldn't get enough of them. He read every page and studied every picture. He just had to learn.

To earn money for food and rent, Fred worked at other jobs at night. He set pins in bowling alleys, cleaned floors in pool halls, and swept grocery stores. He moved from one rooming house to another, staying near the extra jobs he had. His landladies often found jobs for him and paid him with plates of food. Other times, he ate the oranges, apples, or bananas that had been thrown away by grocery stores.

Fred got some of his food from a bakery near Crothers' Garage. The baker chopped up day-old cakes, pies, and cookies, and pressed them into large pans. Then he would cut this mixture into big squares to sell at five cents apiece. Many times, the only food Fred would eat all day would be two of these rich, sweet squares washed down with milk.

Fred bought a pair of long coveralls with some of the first money he earned. He had to get out of those knee pants now that he was working with men. The few clothes he had, Fred washed and patched, over and over. He had better uses for the money he earned than to buy new clothes. During his lifetime, Fred never wanted more than a change of work clothes, two suits, and two pairs of shoes at one time. As long as they were clean (and they had to be that), what more did he need?

A street scene in Cincinnati, showing streetcars and automobiles, around 1900

Riding a streetcar to work one day, Fred noticed that the man in front of him was busy with a two-part ruler. Fred watched, fascinated; then he asked the man what it was.

It was a slide rule. The stranger showed Fred how it could be used to find answers to multiplication and division problems. He explained that most persons who drew plans for buildings and machines used slide rules in their work. Fred decided he'd have to get one.

Luck was with him. Not long after that, Fred met a boy who had found a slide rule on the sidewalk, and he bought it from the boy for ten cents. Fred taught himself to use it, intrigued by how fast he could do complicated mathematical problems. He figured he would use this gadget at the garage when he got around to designing a race car.

One of the cars Fred remembered working on at the Crothers' Garage was the Maxwell automobile.

By the time Fred was really fourteen, Mr. Crothers had made him a full-time mechanic. It seemed to the other mechanics that Fred could just touch a motor and know what was wrong. If he couldn't fix it, he'd study the repair manuals and then explain to everyone else how to do it. By the time Fred was fifteen, he was the foreman.

Crothers' Garage did more than repair passenger cars. Mr. Crothers was involved in automobile racing. The local owners of the latest cars met every weekend at nearby racetracks and hill-climbing sites to see which cars could go the fastest without falling apart. Mr. Crothers owned several racing cars. To advertise his garage, he entered them at the county fair tracks, with banners that read "Crothers' Garage" attached to their sides. Fred spent many Sundays repairing these cars between races.

In his spare time, Fred designed several racing cars, or "speed wagons," himself, which he and the garage crew built. They stripped two autos, an Elmore and an Alco, down to the bare frames of their chassis. Then they pulled the steering posts down to sporty angles and installed foot throttles and bucket seats. The Elmore and the Alco were now ready for the racetrack.

Though seventeen-year-old Fred was old enough to build the cars, Mr. Crothers wouldn't let him race them. He said Fred was too young to compete. It could be that Mr. Crothers didn't want a "colored" boy driving his car at a public event. Although there was no segregation in the repair pits, an African American was seldom given a prominent place as a driver. Fred thought his boss was being unreasonable and unfair.

A big race was coming up at Rising Sun, Indiana, forty miles down the Ohio River. Fred worked night and day, tuning up the two cars. All the while, he hoped he would be permitted to drive in at least one race. A few days before the big weekend, Mr. Crothers assigned two men from his office to drive the cars. He ordered Fred to stay at the garage.

The afternoon before the races, Fred kept his eye on the big garage clock. The ferry for Rising Sun was leaving at five o'clock. Shortly before five, he hung up his greasy coveralls, grabbed his felt hat, and dashed for the boat. Another mechanic would have to close the shop. Fred intended at least to watch his cars race.

Undoubtedly, Mr. Crothers was surprised to see his mechanic at the track. Fred watched all the races, and he saw one of his cars win. After the races were over, Mr. Crothers asked him to drive a car back to Cincinnati. Fred was shocked but pleased.

The next morning, Mr. Crothers told Fred that although he was a good worker, he did not follow orders. To teach him who was boss, Mr. Crothers demanded that Fred take a vacation. He would let Fred know when he could come back to work.

Fred left the garage and hopped a freight train headed south.

On the Move,
South and North

Fred's hope of finding another job as a mechanic faded as he trudged through Kentucky, Tennessee, and Missouri. Even though he had known discrimination in the North, he had still been given a chance to work on cars. In the South, the Jim Crow laws seemed to separate him from both cars and people. He was shunned by most everyone. The black folks thought he was haughty. He didn't speak the way they did. And, if there were any available jobs, they didn't want a stranger from up North getting them.

White folks just considered him another out-of-work colored boy. They laughed when Fred told them he could read and had worked as a mechanic and built race cars. Even with his "education" and experience as a mechanic, Fred was unable to get a job. What could a "colored kid" know about cars and mechanics? He just didn't know his place. Fred couldn't even find a job sweeping a garage to earn eating money.

Fred was often hungry. People took advantage of the skinny kid who asked to work for something to eat. Once he knocked at the back door of a farmhouse, and a bedraggled white woman opened the door. She pointed to the woodpile and told him to chop it up for the stove—then she would give him a meal. The uncut wood was stacked higher than Fred's head. He split about half the wood and, exhausted, walked back to the house and asked for a sandwich to give him the energy to finish.

The woman brought him a jelly sandwich and a half-full tin of milk. She let him know that that was all he would get and he shouldn't ask for more, but he'd better finish chopping that wood. Returning to the woodpile, Fred decided he had done enough work for the food he'd been given. He chopped a few minutes, piled all the wood he had cut around the big uncut chunks, and walked back to the highway.

When Fred reached St. Louis, he walked around the Mississippi River docks looking for work. The regal steamboats with their pipes and paddle wheels drew him as surely as a car garage. The captain of a sightseeing steamboat, the *Robert E. Lee,* hired Fred to help the fireman in the engine room. Fred's job was to keep the firebox under the boiler filled with sufficient coal to keep the fire hot enough to produce the high steam pressure needed to keep the big paddle wheel turning.

Fred liked his job below deck. He was fascinated by the many gauges, the power that came from the steam boiler, and the throbbing of the boat churning through the water. One day, the captain took Fred into the pilothouse and taught him how to read the charts and to navigate the big boat. Fred caught on fast. He learned about the dangers of the river—the sandbars, snags, currents, fog.

The steamship *Robert E. Lee*

Fred stayed with the captain until the boat was docked for the winter. The captain asked him to work on the boat the next spring, but Fred never made it back to the *Robert E. Lee.*

The longer he stayed in St. Louis, doing odd jobs for food, the more Fred realized that this city was no place for him. Working in a garage was what he really wanted to do, and he wasn't going to find such a job in the South. He hopped a freight going north and changed from one train to another until he got to the downtown railroad yard of Chicago, Illinois. As the train jolted to a stop, Fred jumped down from the empty freight car, buttoned his jacket against the cold winter wind, and headed for the nearest street.

Fred walked around the big city spread out along the shore of Lake Michigan. He was thrilled by the rhythmic noise of the cars, trains, streetcars, and boats. Here he would find the work he wanted. He went to garages asking for work, but no one was hiring. Jobs were scarce for everyone, it seemed. Fred took any job he could find to pay for a sleeping room. He scrubbed floors, shoveled snow, washed dishes, and carried trash. That winter in Chicago, Fred learned again what hunger was. Sometimes he just went to the back doors of the mansions along Chicago Avenue, asking for work and food.

Many weeks went by, and Fred began to think that Chicago was not the city for him either. He decided to go back to Cincinnati and tell Mr. Crothers that he had had enough time off. Just as he came to this conclusion, he found temporary work in the Chicago Cadillac Garage. Fred soon amazed the other mechanics with his ability to spot problems and repair machines.

One customer at the garage was Andrew Burke, a wealthy potato grower from northwestern Minnesota. He lived in Chicago in the winter and on his farm in the summer. He liked watching Fred work. Burke told Fred about a neighbor, Walter Hill, who owned a 30,000-acre farm near Hallock, Minnesota. Hill, who had many farm machines and three or four Packard automobiles, was looking for someone who could keep them all in repair. Fred should think about going there.

Fred's job at the Cadillac Garage ended, and again he was knocking on doors asking for work and food. On a hot, windy day in late summer, Fred was walking along Lake Michigan to cool off. He came upon a very old black man, standing on the shore fishing. Nearby was a little shack. The man invited Fred to share in a meal of fish. Fred spent many days with this kind person, learning to catch and cook fish, and sleeping in the shack.

The days spent by the water gave Fred time to think about

what he should do next. Andrew Burke's talk had planted an idea in Fred's mind. He would go back to Cincinnati and spend the winter working at Crothers' Garage, if Mr. Crothers would take him back. Then next spring he might go up to the Hill Farm and look it over. Fred stuck to his plan. He didn't want to spend another cold winter in Chicago. On a rainy night in September 1912, nineteen-year-old Fred Jones left Chicago for Cincinnati on what he thought was an eastbound freight.

It was a damp, cold dawn when Fred was jerked awake by the train grinding to a stop. Fred jumped down from the boxcar. He shouted to a man lugging boxes into the depot, asking him how much farther it was to Cincinnati. The man told Fred that he had been on an Illinois Central train and was now in Effingham, Illinois—over three hundred miles from Cincinnati. There would be no train going east until late that night.

Fred wandered down the street toward a sooty brick building with a sign that read "Pacific House." He walked around to the back and knocked on the door. Charles Siegel Miller, the hotel owner, opened it. Of course, Fred asked if there was some work he could do for a meal. Charles looked at Fred and, ignoring a local law about sending black people on their way, asked the young man what he could do. Fred's answer was that he could fix things. Miller needed someone to fix the furnace. Could Fred do it?

Charles had just sold the hotel. He had bought land in Minnesota and would be leaving soon. Yet he hated to leave the hotel to a new owner with the steam boiler not working and winter coming on. A load of forty new flue pipes had been delivered. If Fred could get the furnace working, Charles would appreciate it.

A view of the Pacific House Hotel and its sign from the train tracks

Fred took a look at the dilapidated furnace. He thought he could fix it, but it would take time. He would catch no train that night.

Fred knew how to fire a boiler from his experience on the steamboat. But he had never fitted flue pipes into a firebox, and he had never done any bricklaying. Fred crawled inside the firebox and inspected it. He backed out and sat down, trying to figure out how to get those old pipes out. A man from a nearby hardware store stopped by to talk to Charles. He told Fred that he could borrow the proper flue tools from his store.

The minute Fred saw the tools, he knew how they should be used. He removed the corroded pipes easily and fitted in all the new flue pipes, making them water-tight.

Next Fred started repairing the firebox. Once again, the man from the hardware store came to the rescue. He showed Fred how to make mortar and use a trowel to put the mortar between the bricks. Fred worked deliberately, taking his time, asking questions, and doing it right. He learned the skills he needed as he worked. When he had the job completed, the furnace looked almost new. The job had taken Fred over a month.

The time to test Fred's work came on a cold day in late October. Fred turned on the pipes that filled the boiler with water. Then he shoveled coal into the newly bricked firebox and watched the gauge atop the furnace gradually move toward the number five, the pressure needed to heat the hotel.

"I didn't know what would happen," Fred said years later. "I half expected that old boiler to blow up the hotel! But luck was with me. It kept heating up, and the flue pipes didn't leak, and the steam started warming the hotel. That job gave me a lot of confidence!"

No one was more pleased by Fred's accomplishment than Charles Miller. He had given Fred a room and all his meals while the young man repaired the decrepit furnace. Now he asked Fred to stay on at the hotel to do more repair work and help the family pack for their move to Minnesota. Fred could come with them to help them get settled on their new farm. There were a lot of people buying farmland up there, and they would need someone to fix machinery.

Charles mentioned that their farm was near a town called Hallock. Fred laughed. Hallock had been his destination that spring anyway.

So it was decided that Fred Jones and Charles's son, Virgil, would ride with the livestock in a freight train. The railroad company, however, permitted only one person to ride with the animals. So Virgil boarded the train with the horses and cows, and then as the freight pulled out to begin its journey north, Fred jumped in. Several times over the eight-hundred-mile trip from Effingham to Hallock, the train crew heard Virgil and Fred talking. But before they got the door opened to check, Fred was hidden in a manger and covered with hay.

At the Farm

On Christmas Day of 1912, in the middle of a blizzard, Fred Jones, Virgil Miller, a few horses, and six head of cattle arrived at the Millers' farm near Hallock, Minnesota. Fred lived with the family of Charles and Bertha that first winter. To earn his keep, he fed the livestock, cleaned the stables, did other chores around the barn, and helped fix up the farmhouse. He listened whenever Charles returned home with supplies from Hallock and something more to tell about the Hill place. This 30,000-acre farm was operated by Walter, the son of James J. Hill—the "Empire Builder"—owner of the Great Northern Railroad.

Besides enormous buildings for equipment, the Hill Farm had an electric generating plant, a water tower, and an immense grain elevator. There were also barns for two hundred horses, shelters with built-in grain tanks for cattle, and a huge hog house. To top it all, Walter Hill owned three big Packard automobiles and a small Packard roadster.

Overall view of the Hill Farm

The more Fred heard about the Hill Farm, the more excited he was to see it. At the end of March, Fred left the Millers and walked several miles over thawing muddy roads to "The Farm." The little town of Northcote stretched along the east side of the railroad tracks, and the Hill Farm, looking almost like another town, stretched out on the west side. Fred crossed the tracks.

He walked around the farm buildings and spied a spacious brick garage near the house. Peering through the windows, he saw the four gleaming Packards. A dream come true.

When Fred spotted the building marked "Office," he went inside to ask for a job. A man with a big western hat tilted back on his head sat behind a huge cluttered desk. His feet, in two ornate cowboy boots, were crossed on top. This was Walter Hill. Half an hour later, after a friendly visit, Fred had a job as a mechanic. The foreman gave him a tour of the farm and told Fred that if he knew anything about fixing machinery, he would be the busiest man in the county.

Late that afternoon, as Fred walked the five miles into Hallock to look for a room, he felt good. Something told him that this was going to be the town where he could stay, a place he could call home.

As it turned out, Fred was right. Along with having a job that was almost more fun than work, he felt comfortable in Hallock. He traveled back and forth to work with other Hill employees. Few of the younger folks in town seemed to care about his color or his Cincinnati-Southerner accent. He played pool and cards, fished and hunted. He fixed up an old saxophone, taught himself to play it, and joined the town band. He went to dances and never lacked a partner.

A panoramic view of Hallock *(top)*; the Hallock Community Band *(bottom)*. Fred is second from the left in the lower row.

Fred Jones soon had three best friends: Clifford Bouvette, whose father owned the local newspaper; Oscar Younggren, a young businessman who owned a garage; and Dr. Arthur W. Shaleen, a physician. These three men were quick to recognize Fred's generous heart and unusual mechanical ability.

Hallock, however, was not free of prejudice. A few of the parents disapproved of their sons and daughters socializing with "that black man." Fred was quiet and respectful around the older citizens, most of whom paid little attention to him. They said that he "kept his place."

Now that Walter Hill had someone to keep the machinery running, he was ready to bring in more modern equipment. He sent Fred by train to Minneapolis in late spring to pick up a huge Reeves steam tractor. On the way back to Northcote, the train's engineer invited Fred to sit in the cab with him. The next Sunday morning, a flat car carrying a giant tractor was pulled off onto a side track at the Hill Farm. Walter and a dozen farmers were waiting. They watched as Fred jumped down from the cab to supervise the unloading.

Threshing on the James J. Hill Farm with the new steam tractor

When the train pulled out, the engineer leaned out of his cab and yelled, "So long, Casey Jones! Take good care of your iron baby!" From that day on, Fred became "Casey" to the people of Hallock and the surrounding towns.

In his felt hat, overalls, blue shirt, and with a 15-cent corn-cob pipe stuck in his mouth, Casey Jones roved the Hill Farm checking his "babies." If he didn't have a repair part for one of the machines, he made one. Sometimes he would study a machine, then look up and say in his southern drawl, "I've got an idea that'll make this work better." Then he'd lay down his pipe, adjust a part or attach a gadget he had made, and indeed it would work better.

One of the men working for Walter Hill at the time was a Great Northern train engineer who had been suspended for not stopping his locomotive at a red signal. Walter told this engineer to teach Fred all he knew about operating a steam engine and electricity so Fred could pass the test required to obtain an engineer's license. Walter intended to invest in the most modern steam machinery, and he wanted his chief mechanical engineer to be certified.

Fred soon discovered how little he knew about the new high-pressure steam engines used for pulling plows and box-cars. But he was an eager student. The engineer coached Fred on all the questions the state inspector would ask. A person was supposed to be twenty-one to get a license. Fred was only twenty, but he looked older. He took the test and passed with flying colors. The state inspector gave Fred his license and said to him, "You aren't as dumb as you look."

This comment didn't shock Fred. He had heard nasty remarks before because of his skin color. He didn't ever let them stop him. Each year, Fred took a more advanced test until he finally earned the highest grade license for a

Minnesota engineer. This was a matter of pride to both Fred Jones and Walter Hill.

One of Fred's favorite jobs was keeping all the Hill Packards in top running condition. The 1912 roadster was Walter's special car. It had two bucket seats in front and one seat in back mounted on top of the gas tank. There were two bars behind the front seats for passengers to hold on to. They needed to hold on—the car's cruising speed was seventy-five miles an hour, and riding in it on the dirt and gravel roads of those days was a thrilling and terrifying experience.

Fred loved this car. He promised himself that he was going to drive a Packard of his own someday, with Frederick McKinley Jones on the registration card. He almost fulfilled that promise the very next year.

Walter Hill drove his roadster wherever he wanted to go, road or no road. He drove out into the fields to watch the men at work or into the pastures to check on his livestock.

One fall day, Walter steered his car off the road and across a ditch in pursuit of a rabbit. The ditch was full of dry straw, and the roadster got stuck. The frantically spinning wheels ignited the straw, and the roadster caught on fire. Walter jumped out. He could do nothing but watch his favorite car burn.

Andrew Burke bought the burned-out Packard from Hill for almost nothing. Then he made a deal with Fred that if he could put it in running order, he could have half interest in the car. Fred didn't care that Andrew's would be the only name on the registration. He worked on that Packard all winter, and by spring, he had it going like new. All that summer, Fred and Andrew took turns driving the roadster around the countryside to dances and ball games.

But the fun of working on Packards and sharing a car

Andrew Burke *(with cap)*, Fred Jones *(middle)*, and another man from Hallock with the fixed-up Packard

didn't last. Walter's father, James J. Hill, died May 29, 1916. As soon as he could, Walter sold the Hill Farm, loaded his Packards and other possessions onto the trains, and moved back to St. Paul, Minnesota. That fall, after the harvest of his potato crop, Andrew Burke moved back to Chicago for the winter, taking the roadster with him. Fred would have to wait for a Packard all his own.

Once again, Fred found himself without a job. Most of the 30,000 acres of the Hill Farm were broken up and sold as smaller parcels. No one needed a full-time mechanic.

During that harvest season, Fred worked with threshing crews in North Dakota, Saskatchewan, and Manitoba. When winter came, he returned to Hallock and got just the job he wanted—in Oscar Younggren's garage.

The Speed Merchant
and Soldier

Oscar, like Fred, was a quiet, thoughtful, inventive man. Unlike Fred, Oscar was a businessman who had acquired his mechanical know-how in schools. These two men had spent many winters talking about cars. Fred had described the race cars he had built and the ideas he had for a better racer. Now Oscar asked him to build it, here in the Younggren Garage. Fred agreed—if he could drive it! Oscar bought a used Dodge touring car, and the two men set to work.

They lowered the body and shortened the frame. The Dodge engine stayed, but they used many parts from other cars and tractors. If they needed a part they didn't have, Fred made it. They used valves from a Hudson super-six to make the engine breathe better and go faster. They chose the rear axle from a Model T Ford for its sturdiness. Fred planed down the engine's cylinder head to obtain higher compression and make the engine run faster. He drilled holes diagonally through the crankshaft to provide better lubrication and give the bearings longer life. The oil pump from a Rumley tractor, driven by the camshaft, force-fed oil to the bearings. The gas tank was moved to the back. Four carburetors were installed, and a special hand pump was attached to the dash so air could be pumped into the gas tank. The driver would have to pump with one hand and steer with the other.

The finished race car was named "15" for the year 1915, when Oscar and Fred had begun to plan the car. Most people called the car *Number 15*. Many of the ideas Fred built into it were not put into other race cars until twenty years later.

Fred *(middle)* with other car lovers in the Younggren Garage

Younggren
Garage *(right)*

While Fred was getting *Number 15* into top racing form, Oscar was putting together a do-it-yourself airplane called a *Curtiss Pusher*. When the men had completed their projects, Oscar had an idea. Why not have a car and airplane race? They could use the track at the fairgrounds—Fred driving *Number 15* and a barnstormer pilot flying the plane.

The next Sunday, more than one hundred spectators were in the grandstand. When the race began, the barnstormer in the plane was at the far end of the field. Fred, in *Number 15,* was at the starting line in front of the grandstand. Someone gave the plane's propeller a spin and jumped out of the way as the motor revved up, and the plane took off. The pilot circled the field once, and as the plane again came over the starting line, four men gave *Number 15* a big shove. The race was on!

Five hundred feet above the track, the plane had no trouble staying ahead of the race car while flying straight down the course. But when the plane got to the curved ends of the track, the pilot had to make a wide turn. Fred shot ahead of the plane. Again the plane overtook *15* on the straightaway. Finally, after ten laps around the track, Fred was declared the winner. *Number 15* was a success. Oscar signed it up for some races at other tracks.

That summer was the kind Fred had dreamed about for a long time. With Oscar and the car, he toured the dirt tracks of county fairs in Minnesota and North Dakota. Fred, a real charger, was often the winner, driving at speeds of almost one hundred miles an hour. Because he knew exactly what his race car would do and was "hot" in the turns, Fred was a skillful and daring driver to watch. Hunched over the wheel, he steered with one hand and worked the air pump with the other. He was a favorite with the cheering crowds. But after this one season of racing, *Number 15* was put in mothballs. The United States had entered World War I.

Young men left their homes and jobs to become soldiers, sailors, and aviators. Yet the farm machines still had to be kept running to harvest the crops for the war effort. "Get Casey!" became the order whenever an overworked piece of machinery gave out. Fred went from field to field, repairing machines and helping farmers harvest their crops. By the end of 1917, however, he had started thinking about joining the armed forces. He enlisted in the 809th Pioneer Infantry, a Minnesota regiment, on August 1, 1918.

Frederick McKinley Jones in the ranks of the United States Army

Fred didn't mind going into the service, but he sure didn't like the idea of a segregated army. Being assigned to an all African American unit reminded him of the time he had spent in the South, where white people and black people stayed away from each other. For most of his life, Fred had lived and worked with white people. He didn't feel black or white, and he didn't like being put in a category.

The army was also the first period in his life since Fred was seventeen years old that he was not his own boss—free to think for himself, to make his own decisions, to do what he wanted when he wanted. Following army regulations and orders was difficult for him.

After training at Camp Dodge, Iowa, Fred's unit was sent overseas. They sailed September 12, 1918, on the *President Grant*. They arrived in France and were assigned to a camp not far from the front lines.

When Fred's commanding officers learned he knew something about electricity, they gave him orders to rewire the whole camp, beginning with the hospital tents. To help him do the job, he was given a group of German prisoners of war. Even with the language barrier, the prisoners understood Fred and vice versa. It was a rather friendly atmosphere. In no time, Fred and the prisoners had the camp "lit up" like it had never been before.

After Corporal Fred Jones had improved the wiring at his camp, he was ordered to other camps to do rewiring. He also kept the telephone and telegraph systems of the camps in working order. At the same time, he repaired the motorcycles of army messengers and the vehicles used to haul men and supplies. Whenever something needed fixing, the order went out, "Get Jones!"

Corporal Fred M. Jones wrote often to his friends in

Hallock. Although he enjoyed his work, Alma Anderson, a young Hallock girl, received a note from him saying, "I'll be glad to be back in God's land." On July 6, 1919, Fred sailed from St. Nazaire, France, and was discharged from the army at Camp Dodge on July 23, 1919.

Back in Hallock, Fred rented a room with space for a shop. He would work at any job electrical or mechanical. His charges varied, usually amounting to just a little more than his expenses.

The doctors in Hallock often asked Fred to drive their cars for them to make country calls. Driving Dr. Shaleen through a snowstorm one day in 1919, Fred decided to make a snowmachine for quicker, easier traveling. He found a discarded airplane body and attached two ski-like runners on the front and two on the back. He attached an airplane propeller to a forty-horsepower airplane engine and mounted the propeller and engine on the back. Over the gas tank, he put an old car seat, and on the front, he added handlebars from a bicycle to steer the back runner. There were no brakes. To stop the machine, Fred and his passenger simply dragged their feet in the snow! The contraption ran, but it could not start or stop on its own. It had to work better than this for Fred to be satisfied.

One January morning in 1921, Fred saw a mail car with skis pull up in front of the post office and brake to a stop. It was a converted Model T. The front wheels had been replaced with skis. Fred's mind raced as he sketched a plan for a new snowmachine. This one would have front steering, brakes, and a car engine.

Fred and his improved snowmachine brought complaints. He was scaring people and horses when he drove that thing through the streets. Soon he was forbidden to operate the snowmachine within city limits. So he hauled it out onto the open prairie, where he could open up the engine to its maximum speed. The whirling propeller whipped the snow into a blizzard as Fred expertly steered the runners over ditches and along barbed wire fences. Cows, horses, and sheep ran for shelter when they heard the machine coming.

Fred's snowmachine with its airplane propeller

Skimming over snow and ice made Fred long again for the excitement of driving a race car. *Number 15,* stored in the back of Oscar's garage, came out of retirement. Using parts from it, Fred built a new race car—lower, lighter, and faster. This one had an aluminum body, wire wheels, and a pressurized gas tank. He removed the starter as well as the low and reverse gears. This made the transmission lighter, requiring less horsepower. But the race car still had to be pushed to get it going. Fred experimented with different mixtures of gasoline and alcohol until he had just the right combination to give the engine more power to run faster.

Fred and *15* were back on the racetrack. For several summers, Fred Jones was a speed merchant again, touring the dirt racetracks from Canada to Texas with *Number 15.* Oscar Younggren went along as business manager. He collected the prize money and saw to it that Fred had sleeping rooms in places where hotels did not accept African Americans.

Fred's reputation grew each summer. He was sometimes billed as the "Speed King" or the "Daredevil." His entry in a race assured ticket buyers an afternoon of thrills. After the races, the spectators would crowd around to see what made *Number 15* the winner time after time.

Although Fred was popular with racing fans, some drivers refused to race against a black man. They would argue with the track manager, but since Fred brought the crowds, the manager would usually say that Casey Jones was driving, and that was that. There were times, though, when all the drivers in a race refused to compete with Fred. Then he would quietly suggest that they all race separately against time, and the driver with the shortest time would win.

Other drivers thought it too dangerous to be on a track with Fred. Those who were not as skillful or as fast-thinking as him sometimes lost control of their cars.

Before a race in Aberdeen, South Dakota, several of the nineteen starters secretly agreed to box in Fred to prevent him from taking the lead and winning. During the race, Fred tried again and again to shoot ahead. Each time, the conspirators crowded around to hold him back. Finally, Fred forced the other cars to the railing and shot around them as they slid toward the fence.

After the dust cleared, five cars had been damaged and one driver had been seriously injured. Fred won the race, and the crowd roared its approval.

Fred had his share of accidents too. Many times, he had to jump to safety. Once at a fair in Hallock, his car flipped over, pinning him down. As men ran to free him, they heard him shout, "Hey, fellas! Get this car off my neck, will ya!"

Fred the speed merchant in *Number 15*

In 1925, Fred was invited by the Motor Racing Association of Chicago to drive in the International Races there. His expenses were paid, and he was to receive part of the winnings. Some of the best speed merchants in the country would be competing.

By late afternoon, the races had reached a fever pitch. Many drivers had been injured, and three had been killed. Just before Fred was to drive in a five-mile race, he noticed that he was walking in blood. Sick, depressed, and nervous, he started his car. On one of the curves, he got too close to the fence. As his car began to roll, he was thrown clear, but he hit his head and was out cold. He regained consciousness in the ambulance. Only his nose was broken.

But the fun had gone out of racing. Fortunately, Fred already had a new passion.

Electronics
Wizard

Fred's friend Clifford Bouvette was now editor of Hallock's weekly newspaper. One day, he had said to Fred, "Casey, do you know that we could talk to people all around the world if we had a wireless?"

Fred hadn't thought about it before, but the idea intrigued him. The wireless telegraph was then the major form of communications over long distances. Messages could be sent to a receiver through a continuous wave (CW) of radio signals. Using the Morse code, dots and dashes were tapped out with a key on the radio transmitter. The key interrupted the sound wave to produce the coded messages.

The young men decided to go over to Dr. Shaleen's office to see if he had any books on electronics and the physics of sound. He did. Using these and buying others, Fred drew diagrams of how to build each unit of the sound transmitter. Cliff suggested they use low-power voltage to make the current safe to handle. Fred just snorted! They would use more power than ships at sea.

The back room of the newspaper office became their shop. Fred and Cliff built a powerful wireless set and put an antenna on the roof. After they had studied and memorized the Morse code, their fun began. They tapped out messages any time of day or night. They sometimes received return messages from operators far away.

A friend told them about a schoolteacher, Professor Curtis, in Pembina, North Dakota, who was supposed to have an exceptionally fine wireless set. He communicated with operators all over the country.

That very night, Fred and Cliff drove the twenty miles from Hallock to Pembina to see the professor. He did indeed know all there was to know about sound transmitters. They listened and watched, never mentioning that they had a set. Professor Curtis informed them that a person had to have a license to operate a wireless station and that to get a license one had to pass a difficult test in electrical engineering. In fact, two men from the federal government were presently in northwestern Minnesota trying to locate an unlicensed set operating there. It was so powerful, he said, that it was interfering with navy communications.

Fred and Cliff left immediately, rushed back to their shop, and took down the antenna. Then they hid the set in a dark corner behind the printing presses.

Two days later, federal officers arrived in Hallock. After two weeks of questioning people and searching buildings, they discovered the unlicensed set. Fred and Cliff were issued a severe warning. The powerful set was left unused and, for a time, forgotten.

Fred's work on that wireless transmitter, though, had left him with another question. What made the transmitter work? He settled down to do some serious studying through

mail-order courses. He never sent back the lessons that came
with the courses, but he laboriously read and studied the text-
books that were delivered. In this way, Frederick McKinley
Jones became an expert in the fields of electronics, the physics of sound, and electrical engineering.

To earn money, Fred worked for himself and others repairing machines. It was said that he could make a balky engine
run better than new. He also built things. Luke Younggren,
a town resident and friend of Fred, said, "Casey built Hallock's first decent fire whistle. He put some Model T Ford
wheels in a drum, got them spinning, then ran compressed
air through it. You could hear that whistle for miles!"

When Fred needed more money for materials and books,
he would repair appliances, wire houses for electricity, build
radios. He advertised in the local newspaper and charged a
small fee for his services, just enough to buy what he needed
at the time. He never had a set fee for anything he did or
built. Having extra money in his pockets seemed like nonsense
to him. Pouring over books, drawing plans, and continually
learning was what interested Fred.

During his years in Hallock, Fred was frequently called
upon by the doctors to make special surgical instruments
and to repair medical tools. In 1923, he was asked to install
the first X-ray machine for the new Hallock hospital. While
he was installing it, Fred came in contact with a high-volt-
age line. The shock knocked him out for several minutes.
His life was saved only because he had been standing, well
grounded, in rubber-soled boots.

Shortly after Fred's accident, Dr. Shaleen began complain-
ing to Fred about having to move his patients so many times
to X-ray them for diagnosis. If only there were a way to get
the X-ray machine to the patient instead of the patient to the

X-ray machine. But that was impossible!

To Fred, building a portable X-ray machine was just another challenge. First he went to the hospital to study the machine that had almost killed him. Then Fred worked out a design on paper. As he drew his plans, he thought about where he could get the material and parts he would need. There was some sheet metal at the Younggren Garage, and he could do the lathe work and welding there. He would get that old sound transmitter from Cliff's place, and the doctors could buy the X-ray tube and electrical meters. Everything else could be made out of odds and ends.

Fred was responsible for all his inventions, and he never let anything he made be tested by or on someone else. Once the small X-ray machine was built, he and Cliff became guinea pigs in testing it. They took picture after picture of the bones in their bodies. In their pictures, some bones appeared distorted, others oblong rather than round. When Dr. Shaleen stopped by and did not mention the odd shapes, Fred asked him what made the bones look so irregular. The doctor told him that all X-ray machines did that. Fred declared that his machine wouldn't!

Fred studied his machine and the pictures, and again read all he could about X rays. He took his time. Fred went over the X-ray machine, changing, adding, adjusting. The testing began once more. This time, film after film showed perfectly formed bones.

Dr. Shaleen declared the machine a work of art. No factory could have done a better job!

Fred's portable X-ray machine, transported from room to room on a little rubber-tired wagon, was used for years in the Hallock hospital. It did not occur to Fred, or to his Hallock friends, to apply for a patent on this invention.

Within a year after Fred built his portable X-ray machine, a similar X-ray machine was being sold in the United States.

Another idea Fred had was to build a small, lightweight radio that used tiny amplifiers instead of vacuum tubes to conduct and expand sound. He drew up plans for the idea, but amplifiers as small as he needed were unheard of. Fred did not have the money to develop them himself, so he was forced to forget the project. Twenty-five years later, three American scientists developed a similar amplifier called the "transistor." This device helped pave the way to the age of the computer.

It was also in 1923 that Cliff came into Fred's shop carrying a huge box. "Casey, did you ever give any thought to building a radio transmitter?" He showed Fred what he had with him: a motor-generator set that had an output of 2,300 volts of direct current. If it were fitted with a microphone and other parts, the set could change sound into electrical signals and send them out through the air. Then they could broadcast from their own radio station.

The two young men went to work. Fred was the teacher, Cliff the student. A little building in Bouvette's backyard became the station, where they built a transmitter about four feet square and six feet high. They used the same kind of microphone all radio stations were using at that time, which produced static and voice distortion. It wasn't good enough for Fred.

At four o'clock one morning, Fred ran to the Bouvette home and pounded on the door. "Come on, Cliff! Let's put this microphone on the railroad track to see if it picks up the sound of the train that's coming this way!" There was a train, the *Winnipeg Flyer,* due in Hallock at six o'clock. Fred's improved microphone, which he called a "condensor type," worked perfectly. The microphone picked up the vibrations traveling down the tracks, and the transmitter broadcast the hum clearly. Later, a device similar to his was patented, and the entire broadcasting world began using it.

Now that they had a radio transmitter and a clear microphone, one of them was going to have to take the test so they could get an operator's license. They decided to talk to the dean of the School of Electrical Engineering at the University of North Dakota in Grand Forks, seventy miles south of Hallock. They needed to find out what they had to know. So Cliff made an appointment for ten o'clock the next Saturday morning.

Before they walked into the dean's office, Fred told Cliff that he must do all the talking. Fred would just listen. Fourteen hours later, Fred and the dean were still discussing, enthused by each other's knowledge of electricity. It was late the next morning when Cliff and Fred finally got back to Hallock. Cliff wrote a letter to the dean asking if he thought Fred was ready for the exam. His reply was "Yes! Fred Jones has the keenest mind of anyone I have ever met."

Between them, Fred and Cliff got together enough money to send Fred to Chicago by train to take the operator's exam. He easily passed all sections of the test. Since Cliff was to be the radio announcer, he applied for the station license. This license gave him permission to use 100 watts of electricity. This, of course, was not enough for Fred. He pushed the power up to 500 watts, allowing the radio waves to be heard 600 miles away.

Cliff went on the air from noon to one-thirty in the afternoon on Mondays, Wednesdays, and Fridays. He reported the local news, personal messages from people in town to people living in remote areas, his views on almost any subject, and always the weather.

One afternoon, Fred joined Cliff for the broadcast. They got into a heated political argument. Fred supported President Warren Harding, an Ohio Republican. Cliff was an ardent Democrat. They began arguing, shouting, and swearing at each other—forgetting they were on the air. The listeners had never heard a program like this! Finally a neighbor ran into the tiny station and threw the switch to cut off the power. The radio audience talked and laughed about the incident for long afterward.

The radio broadcasts from Hallock lasted only a few months. Cliff married and became too busy for broadcasting. He sold the radio transmitter to a station in Moorhead, Minnesota.

A picture postcard of Cliff and Marge Bouvette, shortly after their marriage

Fred, though, kept on building radios for local folks. He ran an advertisement in the Hallock newspaper, the *Kittson County Enterprise*: "Do you want a radio set? If so, I am in a position to build these outfits, which I will guarantee to work to your satisfaction. Signed, Casey Jones."

With his best friend married, Fred began to think about marriage himself. At Saturday night dances, he had met Minnie Hagstrom, a tall, blond Swedish American woman. They enjoyed each other's company, liked to dance, and had a good time together.

When Fred told Cliff that he was thinking of marrying Minnie, Cliff was shocked! An interracial marriage in a small town of conservative people would only bring gossip. The couple would never be accepted. Besides, did Fred want to be responsible for supporting a wife? Fred was thirty years old and set in his ways. How could his work habits and independent nature include a wife? "It will never work!" Cliff told Fred.

As usual, Fred wouldn't listen to anyone tell him something would not work. On September 13, 1923, Fred M. Jones and Minnie B. Hagstrom were married in Hallock by a justice of the peace. Their home was an apartment over the pool hall.

The marriage was in trouble from the beginning. If Fred wasn't out of town, he was working all night in his shop or out drinking with his pals. Fred never had enough money for all that Minnie wanted. Minnie liked to have a good time and companionship, with or without Fred. He was extremely jealous and would lose his temper when he heard talk about Minnie seeing other men.

One night, Fred came home and found Minnie with someone else. He grabbed a kitchen knife and slashed at the stranger as he ran down the steps and out into the street.

Fortunately, only the man's pride was injured.

This event led to the end of a marriage that few people in Hallock even knew about until it was over. Minnie went back to her parents. Fred went back to his life alone, keeping his feelings about the failed marriage to himself.

Then, toward the end of the 1920s, Fred became interested in a fascinating new invention—talking pictures.

Small-Town Talkies

In 1927, Duffy and Geneva Larson became the new owners of the Grand Theater in Hallock. They soon found that people would no longer spend money for silent movies, with subtitles they had to read. In the late 1920s, the Hollywood movie industry had begun making talking pictures. The words and music for the films came on phonograph records that were to be played at the same time as the silent movies. The Larsons couldn't afford the newly fashioned equipment for this. But if they didn't get the talkies, they wouldn't have enough business to pay the mortgage and stay open. Duffy went to Casey. What could be done?

Fred thought about the problem and studied the illustrated advertisements for the new sound-on-disc equipment. An idea began to stir in his head. Fred found two colters (the disc-shaped blades from plows) to use as turntables. He attached a handle on the center shaft of each turntable so that the records could quickly and accurately be moved backward or forward to synchronize with the film. He rigged up some wires so that Geneva could sit at a table in the back of the theater and control the volume.

The Jazz Singer, released in 1927, was one of the first talking pictures.

Fred's sound system turned out to work far better than the one that could be bought. Yet the entire system cost less than one hundred dollars to make.

Fred, however, was the only one who understood how to operate his baby. He would go to the theater just long enough to start the movie. Then, leaving Duffy in charge, he would slip out to work on another project in his shop or in someone's garage. If something went wrong in the projection room, Duffy would round up some little boys who had been watching the movie and order them to "Go find Casey!"

At that time, movies were called "flickers," and that is just what they did. The jerky, flickering way the pictures came onto the screen bothered Fred. So he devised a way to make the pictures steadier and brighter on the screen.

Just as the Larsons were beginning to make some money from the business, a new development came along: sound-on-film. The sound track was now right on the movie film itself. Precise, expensive electronic equipment was needed to convert the sound track into the dialogue, sounds, and music of the picture.

A side view of the Grand Theater in Hallock. One of Fred's workshops was in the basement of the theater.

Duffy and Geneva had no money to buy or rent such equipment. To add to their troubles, some of the ministers in the Hallock churches forbade their members to go to Sunday movies. The Larsons were forced to close the theater on Sunday—the only day when people really had time to see a movie. Was there anything Fred could do?

Here was another challenge. Fred reread his books on electronics. He studied photography. He borrowed books from

Dr. Shaleen on the anatomy of the human eye. What he needed was a lens that could focus a strong, steady light down to the width of a hair. Fred worked out the specifications he wanted for the lens. Then he asked Cliff, who had a new office typewriter, to write a letter to Bausch and Lomb, an optical company, asking them to grind a lens to his specifications. The Bausch and Lomb Company soon answered the letter and sent Fred a variety of lenses. They were unable to grind the lens he wanted, but they wished him success.

Fred always believed that if he wanted something and did not have it, he could make it for himself. His eyes moved over his shop from the front window to the sink in the back. Then he saw his answer—the glass towel rod over the sink! He went to work. From a three-inch slice of the glass rod, he patiently and slowly ground out a tiny lens. When he held this lens between a 100-watt bulb and the wall, he saw a tiny pinpoint of light on the wall. That's what would direct a beam of light through the sound track on the film! The Larsons would help pay for a photoelectric cell and an exciter lamp. Then they could see if Casey's baby would work.

Fred was elated when the cell and lamp arrived. That night, Duffy locked the theater doors, and the two men raced to the projection room to attach Fred's apparatus. All night long, Fred and Duffy worked, connecting, adjusting, focusing the light to the standards of the movie industry—and to the standards Fred set for himself. To cut down on vibrations and to create cleaner sound, Fred draped the ceiling of the theater with gray muslin.

As the town was waking up for breakfast, the men called Geneva. The three of them turned on the projector and heard the dialogue and music of the movie, clearly, distinctly, and in perfect synchronization with the pictures. Fred's machine was a success, even to a perfectionist like himself.

With Fred's new device, the movies were so enjoyable that before long, the Grand Theater became one of the most popular places in the countryside. In a special city election, the people of Hallock voted for Sunday movies, and the ministers were forced to lift their ban and allow church members to go to the movies after evening services. Ticket lines grew longer. After all the seats were taken, moviegoers stood on tables and boxes in the back of the theater. People even sat in the aisles, until the local fire marshal put a stop to this.

News of Fred's marvelous sound system traveled by word of mouth—passed along by salesmen who worked out of Minneapolis. They would schedule their work so they could spend a night in Hallock just to see a movie there.

Joseph Numero, of Ultraphone Sound Systems in Minneapolis, heard about the equipment from a film salesman. The salesman told Joe that a "radioman" or "electrician" had made it, and it "performed excellently." This chance remark brought together two men in an association that would last thirty years.

Ultra Sound Man

Joseph Numero was a very successful Minneapolis businessman, involved in real estate, manufacturing companies, and a finance company. In 1928, he became interested in movie-theater businesses. At this time, Western Electric and Radio Corporation of America (RCA) were the only companies making and installing machines to make the movies talk. Joe and a partner, M. B. Green, decided that it would be a profitable venture for them to start a small company to manufacture affordable equipment for small-theater owners. Ultraphone Sound Systems was born.

Then came the Wall Street panic of October 1929. Stock values plummeted, causing banks and businesses to collapse. The Great Depression began. One of the few businesses that prospered during this period was the motion-picture business. Seeing movies at ten cents for children under twelve and twenty-five cents for adults was a good way for people to take their minds off the hard times.

When Joe Numero heard about the successful homemade sound-on-film equipment being used in Hallock, he wrote to Duffy Larson and asked him to tell that radioman to come to Minneapolis for an interview. At the same time, a Minneapolis broadcasting company, WDGY, heard about Fred's sound system. They sent Fred a letter inviting him to come to Minneapolis to see them about a job, and they included the price of a one-way ticket.

Fred was in a dilemma. He liked living in rural Hallock. It was his home, where his friends were. Would he be able to get used to working in a city? On the other hand, he was thirty-seven years old. Now was the time to leave if he was ever going to do it. Oscar, among many, would miss him, but he still encouraged him to go. "You've got all these ideas going around in your head," he said. "Maybe this will be a way for you to get some money to work on these ideas. If you don't like it there, Casey, you can always come back."

Agreeing, Fred packed a suitcase with a change of clothes, his slide rule, some charts, diagrams, and books. He bought a bus ticket with the money WDGY had sent him. Dressed in a new suit, blue dress shirt, tie, and a new felt hat, with the letter from Mr. Joseph Numero in his pocket, Frederick McKinley Jones got on the bus for Minneapolis. He left behind his home, his friends of eighteen years, and his nickname, Casey.

When Fred Jones arrived at the Minneapolis bus depot, he straightened his tie and started toward WDGY. On the way there, however, he passed the Ultraphone Sound Systems Company and stopped. Going inside, he explained to a secretary that a "Mr. Numero" had asked him to come about a job. When the woman reported this to Joe, his comment was, "We don't have any jobs for a colored boy." But

Fred persisted. He brought out the letter Duffy Larson had received, and that made Joe reconsider. Fred never did make it to WDGY.

Joe took him into the shop, where Fred walked around examining the photocells, projectors, tubes, films, amplifiers. Joe was impressed. When he was called back to the office to answer the phone, he told his six employees to show Fred around. "It was noon before I remembered I had left him in the shop. I hurried out there but saw no one. So I went over to the restaurant where the men usually ate. There they all were, huddled around Fred, listening to him explain something. After lunch, Fred went back to the shop with the men and just took over."

"You know," Fred said later, "when I walked into the shop, I never wanted to leave. I felt the same way I did when I walked into the Crothers' Garage when I was twelve years old. Here in one place was everything I needed to try out the ideas I had going 'round in my head."

Joseph Numero

The other six employees, however, found it difficult adjusting to Fred Jones' peculiar working habits. Fred would leave work to go celebrating at the bars whenever his friends from Hallock visited, spending wildly to give them all a good time. Other times, he would disappear for several days without letting anyone know where he was. A bartender might call Joe in the middle of the night to come get his engineer. Then it would take Fred a few more days to recover, and he would need extra money to carry him over to his next paycheck.

A short time after Fred began working at Ultraphone, Joe reprimanded him about something. Fred exclaimed "Mr. Numero, you didn't hire me, so you can't fire me!"

Joe backed off. He understood the problems Fred was having getting used to living in a large city, handling scheduled work hours, a boss, and a regular paycheck. Joe was willing to be patient for as long as it took Fred to settle down into his new way of life. Numero's partner, M. B. Green, though, saw no sense in Fred's absences, and he resented Joe's overlooking the problems Fred was creating at Ultraphone. Several months after Fred's arrival, while Joe was away on business, Green fired Fred.

Fred was depressed. His only choice was to return to Hallock a failure. And that also meant leaving all the new electrical gadgets he was working on.

When Joe Numero returned, he and Fred made a deal. M. B. Green would no longer be Fred's boss. Joe would look after Fred for the rest of his life. He would furnish Fred with an apartment and pay him enough salary for his expenses. Joe would also pay doctor bills and help out when Fred ran out of money. Fred would have a place to work on his ideas and all the materials he needed. In return, the company would own whatever Fred developed, including the rights to any patents he might receive.

There was no contract to sign. The deal was made with a handshake. Now Fred could spend all his time experimenting and developing ideas without having to bother about money.

The deal seemed to work for both of them. As time went on, Joe Numero was continually amazed by the extensive technical knowledge of his newest employee. "Fred took to the sound-on-film equipment like a duck to water," Joe said. "We were purchasing amplifiers from a large manufacturer, but Fred persuaded me to let him tinker around and make his own. Over my partner's objections, I did. The result was an amplifier with a greater range of both high and low frequencies, and with speakers that distributed the sound throughout the entire theater."

By late 1932, Western Electric and American Telephone & Telegraph (AT&T) initiated lawsuits against Ultraphone, claiming that Fred's sound system had been developed from their patents. They hired a large staff of patent attorneys, scientists, and engineers to testify. The only expert Joe could get to testify was Professor Ballard of Cornell University, recognized as an authority in sound engineering. He and Frederick McKinley Jones were the Ultraphone witnesses.

Before the trial was over, Fred had gained the respect of the judge, the attorneys, and the witnesses for both sides. The AT&T experts were awed by Fred's knowledge and insight into the physics of sound waves and electrical engineering. With no background or schooling, with no Bell Laboratory to experiment in, he had perfected amplifier circuits far superior to theirs.

The lawsuits, however, would drag on for eight years and

be a financial strain on Ultraphone Sound Systems. The suits were eventually dropped, with no company the winner. To keep up with expenses during the long trial, Ultraphone began building and selling theater seats, arc lamps, and a new invention of Fred's—a ticket-dispensing machine. Fred applied for a patent on this invention, which he eventually received on June 27, 1939. It was the first patent granted to him alone.

While waiting for the patent, Joe had another idea to expand Ultraphone business. He asked Fred what he thought about air-conditioning theaters. Here was another challenge!

Off to the Minneapolis Public Library Fred went. He borrowed books and spent many days and evenings studying, checking, making notes, drawing sketches—putting together concepts and ideas about air-conditioning and refrigeration. He found that a refrigeration compressor worked almost the same way as his old friend, the gasoline engine. The difference was that the compressor did not need spark plugs.

As it would turn out, Fred never had a chance to apply his knowledge to air-conditioning a theater. A golf game would send him off on another path.

A lumberjack buys his child a theater ticket in 1940. A copy of Fred's patent for the ticket-dispensing machine *(inset)*

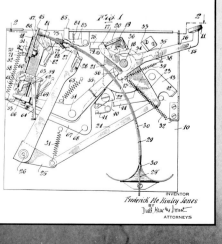

Cool Movers

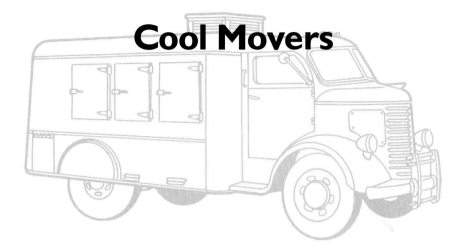

One hot Thursday in May 1938, Joe Numero was playing golf with Harry Werner, head of the Werner Transportation Company; Al Fineberg, president of the United States Air Conditioning Company; and Max Winter, a Minneapolis businessman. During the game, Harry received a phone call that upset him so much it ruined his golf score that day. One of his big transport trucks had broken down on its way to Chicago, and its entire load of poultry had been spoiled. The ice and salt in the truck were no match for the summer sun. Disgusted with his loss, Harry lashed out at Al. "If you guys can cool off a big movie theater, you ought to be able to rig up something that could keep a truck load of chickens from spoiling!"

"We've tried to refrigerate trailers, Harry," Al explained, "but when we put mechanical refrigeration on the road, the jarring and jolting of the truck knocks the whole thing apart. That kind of equipment works only in a stationary object.

Besides, where are you going to get enough electrical power while you are driving down the highway?"

To tease Al a little, Joe laughed and said, "Harry, if Al here can't cool your trucks, I will. I'll put a generator on the wheel of the trailer."

"It's nothing to joke about, Joe!" Al said with disgust. "I suppose your man Jones could make a machine for Harry's trailer!"

"Of course, he could," Joe said with a smile. "If you don't think you can handle it, Harry can call me on Monday and we'll build him one!"

Harry Werner did call Joe on Monday. He had just purchased a new twenty-four-foot trailer, and he was having it delivered to Joe, ordering him to "Put that refrigeration unit on it that you were bragging about last Thursday."

When the trailer arrived, Fred and a couple of sound-on-film assistants crawled all over and under it, taking measurements of the walls, doors, and ceilings. After thirty minutes, Fred announced, "We ought to be able to fix up something, Mr. Numero."

Now, besides their work on the ticket-dispensing machine and sound systems, Joe and his employees worked after hours helping Fred "fix up something" for Harry Werner.

Years earlier, when Fred had been building race cars, he had devised ways to make the car bodies shockproof, to withstand intense vibrations. Now he applied these ideas to design a refrigeration unit that could withstand the vibrations of a jouncing trailer on a rough road. Fred's design called for a four-cylinder gasoline engine that would drive the compressor of the refrigeration unit. He built a combination starter/generator/flywheel that would stop and start the engine automatically. It would also kick the thermostat on and off to keep the temperature inside the trailer steady. Fred put all of the equipment together into a 2,200-pound single unit. "A big clunk," Fred called it. To save storage space inside the trailer, Fred attached the big clunk underneath the trailer.

Fred rode along on the trial run. The unit did not work as efficiently as he had hoped, but the trailer did stay cool. Fred knew he was on the right track. He redesigned the unit, this time using more lightweight materials. It was much sturdier, more compact, and 400 pounds lighter. Again he mounted it under the trailer. The new unit performed so well Fred gave his consent to put it into production. Through Joe's patent attorney, Frank A. Whiteley, a patent for the vehicle air-conditioner was applied for in the names of Joseph Numero and Frederick M. Jones. Before long, the Ultraphone company began manufacturing refrigeration units for truck trailers. Thirty-three units of "Model A" were sold in 1939. The success of these very first units was enough to whet the appetites of the grocery businesses for fresh foods.

In those days, grocery stores were small. Most of the fruits and vegetables sold were canned. Fresh produce was available only during growing seasons and could only be transported short distances. The transport trucks for fresh meats, eggs, fruits, and vegetables used big blocks of dry ice and salt to keep the food cool. But if the truck had mechanical trouble on the road, the ice would melt away and the food would soon spoil. Fred's invention changed everything. Grocers were quick to realize what this invention could mean to them—better, fresher food and more variety for their customers, and thus, more business.

Joseph Numero was now no longer interested in the theater business. He saw that transport refrigeration was a pioneering venture that could turn into a highly successful business of its own. He sold the Ultraphone company, Fred's electronic sound track, and his ticket-dispensing machine to RCA.

To expand production of refrigeration units, Joe borrowed on his life insurance and purchased an entire building in Minneapolis. The first two floors became the office and factory. The upper floor was made into an apartment for Fred. Additional workers were added to the original six Ultraphone employees. Joe called his new business the "United States Thermo-Control Company." The first units were called "Thermotrol," which was soon changed to "Thermo King." Eventually the name of the company itself was changed to the Thermo King Corporation.

Though Joe was confident about Fred's refrigeration units, Fred was not yet satisfied. They should work better than they did. What was wrong? He went back over his design and studied the way the unit had been attached. Soon he saw the answer. The unit would not work dependably as long as it was mounted *under* the trailer. The heat, dirt, mud, and flying pebbles from the road were creating friction and cutting down efficiency. Fred decided to mount his baby high on the trailer's front. Joe said, "Impossible!" Fred retorted, "Nothing's impossible!"

Fred began drawing out his plan. He would turn the starter motor inside out. The stationary part would be inside, and the revolving part would be on the outside. By building the revolving part heavy enough, it could be used as a flywheel as well. With fins on it, the flywheel would work like a fan to keep the engine from overheating.

Fred's new design was built. Instead of putting all of the equipment into one big unit, Fred divided it into two separate chambers. The larger was mounted high on the outside of the trailer. Into this went the gas engine, the compressor, and the condensor: all the heat-producing parts. The smaller chamber was put inside the van, where perishable produce was stored. Into this chamber went the apparatus that withdrew heat from inside the van, cooled the air, and forced the cool air into and through the storage space. Fred's new model weighed about 950 pounds.

It worked! Thermo King soon became the leader for supplying trailers with front-mounted units. No other company's design was as serviceable as Fred's.

A produce truck with two Thermo King cooling units on top

Now that Thermo King had successfully developed a reliable way to transport perishables at controlled temperatures, a whole new industry—the frozen-food business, and eventually the supermarket—was launched. Companies had begun to freeze foods on a small scale by 1939, but they couldn't keep the temperatures cold enough in the truck trailers for the frozen products to be shipped. Now with the invention of Fred's temperature-controlled transport, the frozen-food industry immediately expanded. Frozen food could now be shipped reliably up to distances of several thousand miles. It became possible for people everywhere to eat vegetables, fruits, eggs, poultry, meat, and dairy products at any time of the year. To meet the demands for these foods, many small grocery stores grew or were replaced by sprawling supermarkets. The variety of foods that these huge stores could stock soon included imports from as far away as Hawaii, South America, and New Zealand. Fruits and vegetables previously unavailable to most people became part of their daily diets.

When the United States entered World War II, in December 1941, there was a desperate need for portable refrigeration units to get food and medicine to the troops at the war fronts, and to cool the planes carrying wounded soldiers to hospitals. The Defense Department needed the advice of experts on what equipment would be best for the army to use. The government called the nation's leading refrigeration engineers to Washington, D.C., to present their designs. Fred Jones was invited, of course. However, because he was black, Fred could not stay in the best downtown hotel where the other engineers stayed. He had to register in a lesser hotel reserved for African Americans.

The presentations and discussions of the refrigeration designs went on for days. Finally, the decision was made: the lightweight, compact unit designed by Frederick McKinley Jones of Thermo King would be the standard equipment of the armed forces.

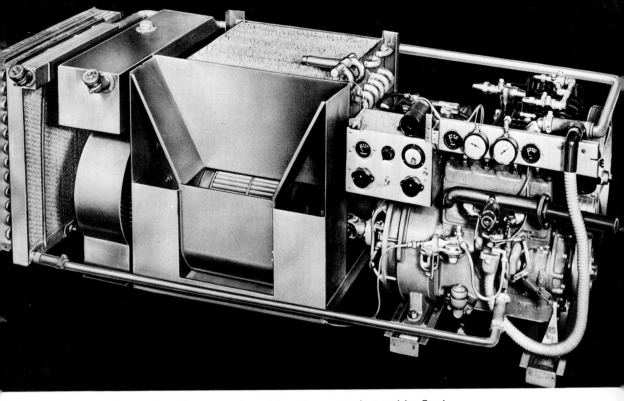

One of the first portable refrigeration units designed by Fred

Large and small models of Fred's unit were sent to combat zones in Europe, Africa, and the South Pacific. They were often dropped in sections from planes or helicopters to the waiting troops. In minutes, a hot and tired soldier could have the unit together and be drinking iced water. Ice-cream machines were made from smaller adaptations of Fred's invention. Other units held perishable foods, serums, drugs, and blood plasma that had to be kept at exact temperatures. Thermo King units were used to cool field hospitals as well as the cockpits and engines of ambulance planes.

To keep up with its government defense commitments, Thermo King expanded its workforce. At Fred's request, several men and women from Hallock were given jobs.

Stanley Grunewald, a young draftsman from Dunwoody Institute in Minneapolis, was also hired. For the next seventeen years, he and Fred Jones shared an office at Thermo

King. Fred wanted his draftsman right beside him. It was Stanley's job to draw the designs of Fred's ideas. Stanley said that Fred always started at the top with the finished idea. Then he "worried" himself down through it to the pieces.

Frances Brewer, Joe Numero's secretary, said of Fred, "One time I brought a passionflower to the office and I told him about the amazing flower with movable parts. His gentleness in examining the construction of that fragile flower was heart-warming."

Fred *(third from right)* working with Thermo King engineers. Stanley Grunewald is on the far right.

Not all employees liked Fred. Some complained that Jones expected them to do things that were not even in books. Fred would tell them that what they were doing would be in the *next* books. He was especially demanding of the African American employees. He wanted them to achieve as he had, through hard work and learning.

Fred had a photographic memory, and he thought everybody he worked with had a mind like his. Still, he was a quiet, patient teacher when explaining a new concept. He just wasn't as patient when something went wrong.

Some employees believed Fred could "smell trouble." If something went wrong anywhere in the plant, Fred sensed it. Out of his office, he would charge, heading straight for the problem. He spent weekends prowling through the plant alone, examining others' work, collecting imperfect parts to show Joe on Monday mornings. When Joe would ask Fred if he wanted the employee who had made the mistake fired, Fred's answer was always, "Fire him! What for? There's nothing wrong with the man—just with what he did!" Yet later he would ask the worker if he had a "bee-bee brain."

Stanley remembered one argument between Fred and Joe. The two men ended up shouting at each other, and Joe walked out of the office. Well, that's the end of that partnership, Stanley thought. He had seen disagreements between the two men, but never one as heated as this. Ten minutes later, Joe stuck his head in the office door and said in a matter-of-fact tone of voice, "Now don't forget, Fred, that we're meeting tonight for dinner."

Although Thermo King filled a large part of Fred's life, there were lonely times when he longed for companionship. He did not socialize with coworkers after they left the plant. When Fred left the building, he would go fishing alone or to a bar. While doing some work on a refrigerated laboratory at the University of Minnesota, he met a young woman associated with the graduate school. Sadly, just as they were becoming good friends, she was killed in an accident.

When the National Elks Club Convention was held in Minneapolis during the summer of 1945, some Thermo King friends talked fifty-two-year-old Fred into going with them. That evening, Fred met Louise Lucille Powell. Lucille was a thirty-two-year-old widow with a teenage son, Tate. She worked as a display manager for several St. Paul stores. Her mother was of French-German ancestry, and her father was Jewish. Lucille was attracted to the tall, handsome, soft-spoken Thermo King engineer.

Fred noticed Lucille's dark, sparkling eyes and her expressive face as she talked and laughed with friends. They made plans to see each other again and soon found time for dinners, drives around city lakes, and quiet times. As Lucille came to know Fred, she grew concerned about his health and work habits. Fred began calling her "Ma" or "Mama" whenever she told him to take care of himself. Fred never asked Lucille to marry him. He just started saying, "When we are married, Mama..."

Fred and Lucille married in 1946, a year after their first meeting. Lucille did not want to live in the apartment above the plant, but she moved there to please Fred.

For the first time, Fred had an orderly, peaceful home. He was content to stay in the Thermo King building all day, every day. About the only time he would leave was when he needed a haircut. When he found that Lucille could cut his hair, he seldom left.

Besides loving his wife and home, Fred was especially

pleased to have a son. He began planning for Tate's college education immediately. But three months after the wedding, Tate died suddenly of leukemia. There had been no hint of his illness before the marriage. Fred grieved with Lucille.

Lucille and Fred Jones

Later she wanted to adopt a child, but Fred refused to consider it. Lucille was desperate then to have something to do and wanted to go back to work. Fred's take-home pay at that time was $38 a week. They could have used a second salary. But Fred refused to consider this idea either. He wanted Lucille there whenever he climbed up to their apartment from the plant. Knowing how important this was to him, Lucille gave in.

Shortly after their marriage, Lucille realized that Fred would give away any money he had in his pockets to any fellow employee who asked for it, so she put herself in charge of Fred's paychecks. Each day when he went downstairs to the plant, she would give him some change for a snack.

When Lucille suggested Fred ask for a raise, he refused to discuss it. Instead he asked her to save enough from his present checks so he could someday own a Packard—which she did. He eventually bought a beautiful dark green Packard Patrician. To the salesman's surprise, Fred paid in cash.

One of their first trips in the new Packard was to Hallock to visit Cliff and Oscar. On later trips up north, the Joneses would often stay for several days in the Younggrens' cabin at nearby Lake Bronson. Sitting on the dock and fishing, four hundred miles from Thermo King, was a favorite pastime. There Fred could truly relax. He loved to fish. It often brought back memories of fishing with his old friend in Chicago.

On quiet evenings at home, the couple listened to music. Fred liked Irish ballads and the classics, especially Chopin. Even in music, Fred was looking for how the different parts worked. "Listen to how the music fits together, Ma," he'd say.

Since the time of his marriage, Fred had been working on another "cooling" project for Thermo King. He decided that his self-contained portable unit would make refrigeration practical for railroads. So for the next several years, Fred experimented to figure out a way to keep food fresh while it was transported by rail.

Fred had boxcars custom-built with refrigeration units and double walls, between which he placed automatic dampers. Air was blown through the dampers and over the perishable cargo. A thermostat opened and closed the dampers to keep the temperature constant. The air inside the boxcar became saturated with moisture, which kept the produce fresh and prevented wilting. These "Atmosphere Control" boxcars were tested from 1948 to 1950.

During these two years, Fred rode 250,000 miles in trains, seeing for himself how his method of boxcar refrigeration worked. Not one pound of cargo was lost from poor refrigeration.

Joe and Fred check out one of the Thermo King boxcar refrigeration units.

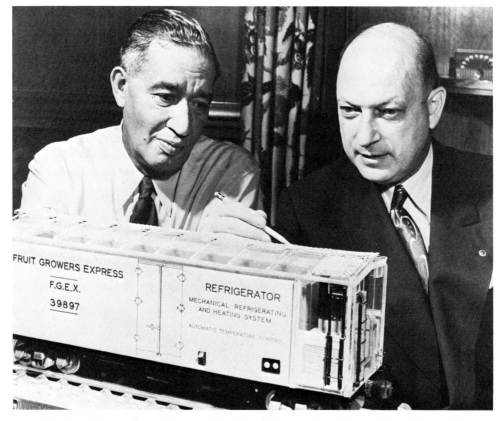

Fred and Joe posing with a model of the Thermo King "Atmosphere Control" boxcar

When Fred saw how perishables could be moved so quickly by simply switching refrigerated boxcars to other railroad lines, he came up with the idea of "containerization." He designed refrigerated trailers or containers that could be easily lifted by cranes onto flat railroad cars, or the decks of ships, or the beds of semitrailer trucks. When the cargoes on railroads or ships reached their destination, the containers could be shifted onto waiting trucks and transported to where the produce was needed. Containers that were shipped overseas were often emptied at the docks, then filled with import products and put back on the ship to be sent to the United States. Containerization was to become the chief method of moving goods of all kinds around the world.

His idea was a success, but Fred's years of long workdays, short nights, irregular meals, and chain smoking had begun to catch up with him, causing serious health problems. The years of getting in and out of refrigerated boxcars and the many miles of travel only aggravated these problems.

Fred at work

After a case of pneumonia and gall-bladder surgery, the doctors ordered Fred to slow down. But Fred had always had trouble relaxing and sleeping. He would go to bed exhausted, yet his mind would not stop working. He often sat up all night, smoking, drawing plans, calculating, figuring. "My head is like a machine," he would tell Lucille. "It won't let me rest. If only I could turn it off!" When he was desperate for sleep, he would go on a weekend drinking binge, then spend a few days sleeping. This happened once every six or eight months. It was the only time Fred did any drinking after he married Lucille.

Joe decided that since Fred was having health problems, he should take out an insurance policy on Fred, with himself as the beneficiary. During the required physical exam, however, the doctor found that Fred was diabetic. The engineer could not be insured. Fred was put in the hospital and started on insulin, which he had to take the rest of his life.

The doctors urged Joe to get Fred away from the Thermo King plant. So Joe bought a summer house on Lake Minnetonka, fifteen miles from the city, for Fred and Lucille to use during the warmer months. Sitting on the dock and fishing became their favorite hobby. Joe and his wife, Blanche, and the Numeros' boxer dogs often joined them there.

The Jones and Numero association was more than an employee-employer relationship. Blanche frequently asked both Fred and Lucille to visit them, and the two wives became close friends. Joe, however, was more distant. He himself never invited the Joneses to his home.

Fame, But No Fortune

By the 1950s, Fred's reputation as an inventor, engineer, idea-man, troubleshooter, and expert mechanic had gained national attention. Articles about his accomplishments began to appear in magazines. Fred was unimpressed. He thought people must have better things to do than write about him. When he was invited to become an honorary member of the American Society of Refrigeration Engineers (ASRE), he resisted. But the Thermo King engineers who were already members insisted. Thus, Frederick McKinley Jones became the first African American to become a member of the ASRE.

One spring, Fred was invited to attend the graduation exercises at Howard University in Washington, D.C., to receive an honorary doctorate. He was surprised. He admitted to Lucille that "Doctor" would look nice in front of his name, considering that he had spent only four years in a classroom. Lucille encouraged Fred to accept the degree. Fred thought it over. "If I go to Washington to get that piece of paper, will it make me any smarter?" He decided not to make the trip.

Frederick McKinley Jones, Vice-President of Engineering at Thermo King

Even so, Fred often regretted his lack of a formal education. He had learned all he knew the hard way and wondered what he could have accomplished with more schooling. It was not the degree or status that he regretted, it was just what he could have learned while earning the degrees. Yet he was not impressed with some of the university-trained men with whom he worked. The men Fred liked to hire were the men who enjoyed dirtying their hands by taking apart machines and asking "How can we make them better?" He often prowled race tracks and garages looking for such men.

Fred never stopped getting his hands dirty, checking his "babies."

One event in his honor Fred did not mind attending was "Casey Jones Day," held at the Kittson County Fair in June 1950. Cliff Bouvette gave the event front-page coverage. "Casey Jones will be an auto race starter at Fair....Fred Jones, a 'Hallock Boy', is rated as the greatest colored scientist in America...a black Thomas Edison."

Joe ordered Fred not to go there and drive in a race. He might be injured or even killed! Fred just chuckled. He did, however, take a new race car—*Number 8*—and a professional driver with him to Hallock. With his old friends standing around, Casey checked over the race car, started the engine, listened to it, and then laughed as he laid his hand on the spark plugs to kill it. That afternoon, Fred hunched his big frame into the small racer and drove slowly around the track where he had first driven *Number 15* more than thirty-five years before. He let the professional car driver take his place in the races.

Scenes from "Casey Jones Day" at the Kittson County Fair, June 1950. Oscar Younggren is on Fred's right in the lower photos.

Fred takes a spin around the Kittson County Fair track in the race car made especially for Casey Jones Day.

In 1953, Fred was presented the Merit Award of the Phillis Wheatley Auxiliary, a settlement house in Minneapolis for young African Americans. Fred was cited for his "outstanding achievements which serve as an inspiration to youth." After the presentation, Fred thanked the auxiliary for the honor. Then to everyone's surprise, he gave a short speech. In his slow, deliberate way, he told his large audience of young people how to achieve goals in their lives.

There are three things to do to become successful, he told them. First, don't be afraid to get your hands dirty. Don't be afraid to work. Try lots of jobs. Work for nothing if you have to, but get the experience. You never know when what you have learned will come in handy.

Second, you have to read. Find out what others know. You don't have to buy books. Use libraries! You can educate yourself by reading. All my life has been study and work. That's what I get fun out of.

And third, you have to believe in yourself. If you think you're right about something, don't listen to others tell you you're wrong. Remember nothing is impossible. Go ahead and prove you're right.

Fred had had to believe in himself. Many who worked at Thermo King and others from all parts of the country who came to Thermo King on business did not look at Fred as a professional engineer, nor as their social equal. Even though Joe Numero recognized Fred's skills, he never considered Fred a business or social equal either. Fred's wide-ranging interests, friends, and contacts always surprised Joe.

During a business trip to Washington, D. C., Fred stopped the taxi in front of a large office building because he said he knew somebody in there he wanted to see. "I went along," Joe said, "thinking Fred's friend was a janitor or a doorman. We went up to one of the top floors and as we walked out of the elevator into a huge office, a tall, dignified man came out of an inner office and yelled, 'Casey!' Fred shouted, 'Art!' and the two men put their arms around each other and went back into Art's office. I found out that Art was Arthur Anderson, Treasurer of the United States Export-Import Bank. He was born and raised in Hallock." Joe found it amazing that Fred would know anyone of national power and prestige.

Arthur Anderson, though, was proud to tell people that he, like Fred, was a graduate of "H.P.O.," the Hallock Post Office. He had educated himself by taking correspondence courses.

Art Anderson, Treasurer of the U.S. Import-Export Bank, poses in Washington, D.C., with his friend Fred Jones.

As Fred's reputation as an inventor and expert engineer grew, he was offered jobs in other companies, for very large salaries. "Leave Thermo King and my babies to take another job?" Fred snorted, "Just for money?" He never even considered it.

Fred's loyalty to Thermo King, though, seemed strange to some people, including, at times, Lucille. Although Fred's inventive genius helped to build Thermo King, he owned no part of the company. There were no signed contracts or stock certificates in Fred's name. Fred's sixty or more patents were the property of Thermo King because they had been developed there. His title was Vice-President of Engineering, yet the highest salary Fred received was $12,000 a year, near the end of his life.

During the mid-1950s, poor health began to keep Fred in bed more and more. Through many hospitalizations, operations, and illnesses, Fred continued to work out plans with Thermo King for the many new ideas that were constantly coming to him.

He predicted that the time was coming when all automobile manufacturers would be forced to build gas engines in a way that would cut down or eliminate pollution. He began designing a revolutionary engine, an improved version of a two-cycle gas engine for which he had received patents in 1945 and 1946.

Another of Fred's ideas had to do with home heating and cooling. He had promised Lucille that someday they would build a home with no furnace. Fred wanted to pump water out of the ground and use it for heating the house in winter and air-conditioning it in summer. He told Lucille that as long as water was liquid there was heat in it. This was a new concept in home heating, an idea that Fred did not live to develop.

In 1956, Thermo King moved to its huge new plant in Bloomington, Minnesota. Although Fred had designed the research division of the plant, he was too ill to even visit the facility. But many from Thermo King came to him. Stanley Grunewald visited Fred twice each week for four years, keeping him posted on what was going on at the plant. Together they worked on plans for the more pollution-free gas engine, as well as on improvements to products already being made. Stanley would take Fred's ideas, designs, and orders back with him to Thermo King.

In 1957, Fred and Lucille bought a house in south Minneapolis. Fred was too sick to see the house before moving in. He spent the last four years of his life in bed at his new home or in a hospital. Fred disliked being in hospitals, and when he was at home, he refused to use a hospital bed. Instead, he designed an apparatus that could be attached to his own bed to lift his weakened body up and down. Stanley took the plan and had it made for Fred back at the plant.

Fred underwent surgery for the removal of a brain tumor in 1960. But even that did not stop his head from "running like a machine." Ideas still poured from his mind, and he continued to calculate, figure, and draw plans. Doctors who came to know Fred were fascinated by his mind and by his great interest in medicine. Medical specialists would often go to Fred's home to see how he was, and they would remain for hours to exchange ideas with "that remarkable man, Fred Jones."

Among Fred's other frequent visitors was Lucille's nephew, Billy, who talked to Fred shortly before his death. During that last visit, Fred said to Billy, "I've been a lucky man. I've done all the things I wanted to do."

On February 21, 1961, Fred Jones died from lung cancer. He was sixty-eight years old.

Fred was to be buried at Fort Snelling as a veteran of World War I. On the way from the mortuary to the fort, the long funeral procession stopped before the new Thermo King plant—the plant that Fred had never seen. On that subzero winter day, hundreds of employees gathered on the Thermo King mall in a last tribute to Frederick McKinley Jones.

Afterword

Soon after Fred's death, Joe Numero sold the Thermo King Company. It is now a subsidiary of Westinghouse Corporation. More than 40,000 square feet of space are dedicated to the Engineering Research and Test Center, and engineers there are still working on improvements to Fred's ideas. He would be pleased that the researchers are now designing units that will work with alternative refrigerants to protect the earth's fragile ozone layer.

On September 16, 1991, Frederick McKinley Jones and Joseph Numero were posthumously presented with the National Medal of Technology. Jones and Numero were the first persons in the medal's history to be given the award after their deaths. Their widows, Lucille Jones and Blanche Numero, were presented the medals by President George Bush in the Rose Garden of the White House.

Frederick McKinley Jones was also the first African American to be recognized by the United States government with the National Medal of Technology. His inventions have contributed vastly to raising the quality of life of people all over the world.

Notes

page 8—No birth certificate for Frederick McKinley Jones exists. Since it is likely that Fred's parents never married, Fred's middle name, McKinley, may have been his father's last name, and Jones may have been his mother's last name. Fred could also have acquired his middle name in his early years when William McKinley was president.

page 10—Fr. Edward A. Ryan was pastor of St. Mary's parish in Hyde Park, Cincinnati, 1901–1905. There was no parish parochial school until 1904. We assume that Fred probably attended a public school.

page 29—The song about Casey Jones and his Cannonball Express was being sung all over the country. Many do not know that the man who wrote the song was Wallace Saunders, an African American who was a roundhouse worker and a friend of the real Casey Jones, who lost his life in the fabled train wreck.

page 46—The three American scientists who developed the tiny amplifier called the transistor were John Bardeen, Walter H. Brattain, and William B. Shockley. They received the Nobel Prize in physics in 1956 for this accomplishment.

page 76—Lucille Jones kept a journal of Fred's recollections of his early life. Many of the facts in this book were originally based on Fred's memories.

page 82—Fred would have smiled when three race cars, sponsored by Thermo King, qualified for the "Indy 500" on Memorial Day, 1967. The Thermo King race car driven by Mel Kenyon was named *15*.

page 89—In Thermo King's 50th year, 1989, a scholarship fund was established in Fred's memory. The Westinghouse Foundation presented $50,000 to the University of Minnesota Institute of Technology to be used for minority students pursuing degrees in mechanical engineering. The university matched this gift, making a $100,000 lasting endowment.

page 89—Joseph Numero died on May 8, 1991, at age 94.

Bibliography

Primary Sources

Numerous interviews with Fred's friends in Hallock and at Thermo King.

Bouvette, Clifford. One of Fred's best friends in Hallock. Personal interviews and written remembrances.

Buske, Don H. Archivist, Archdiocese of Cincinnati. Letter, confirming that there was a Fr. Ryan as Fred remembered.

Grunewald, Stanley. Fred's draftsman at Thermo King.   Personal interviews.

Jones, Lucille. Wife of Frederick McKinley Jones. Personal interviews and written recollections.

Larson, Geneva. Personal interviews.

Leitzell, Lulu. Daughter of Charles S. Miller. Letters to the authors in 1970.

Numero, Joseph. Chairman of the Board, Thermo King. Personal interviews.

Shaleen, Margaret. Wife of Dr. Shaleen, Hallock physician. Letter, 1970.

Snyder, Bill. Race car driver, brought by Fred to Thermo King. Interview.

Whiteley, Frank A. Patent lawyer. Correspondence and patent applications.

Younggren, Josie. Oscar Younggren's wife. Interviews. Her cabin on Lake Bronson was a favorite place for Fred and Lucille to relax and rest.

Secondary Sources

"American Inventor Holds More Than 40 Patents for His Processes in Refrigeration." *Iraq Times,* July 29, 1953.

Edgerton, Jay. "Crack Engineer Shuns Praise." *Minneapolis Tribune,* May 4, 1949, 21.

"Frederick McKinley Jones, Black Genius." *Effingham (IL) Daily News,* March 1, 1947. Collected in *Gopher Historian,* Fall 1969, 1.

Hallock: A History of Our First 100 Years. Compiled as a Centennial Project in 1983. Grafton, ND: Associated Printers, 1983.

Hiebert, Gareth. "His Inventions Live On." *St. Paul Pioneer Press,* June 5, 1971, 1.

History of Kittson County in the World War, 1917–1918–1919. Pipestone, MN: The Leader Publishing Company.

"Honors for Twin Citians." *Minneapolis Star Tribune,* September 4, 1991.

Kittson County and Red River Valley Historical Societies. *Our Northwest Corner. Histories of Kittson County, Minnesota.* Dallas, Taylor Publishing Co., 1976.

Kittson County Enterprise. Many items from the weekly editions and from the *Fiftieth Anniversary Number, 1935.*

"New Units 'Melt' Freight Car Dry Ice." *The Christian Science Monitor,* March 16, 1951, 1.

Reasons, George and Sam Patrick. "They Had A Dream. F. M. Jones—Invented Cooling System." *The Evening Star,* Washington, D. C., March 28, 1970.

Spencer, Steven M. "Born Handy." *Saturday Evening Post,* May 7, 1949.

Thermo King Messenger. Various issues in 1960 and 1961, and other recent publications from Thermo King Corporation.

Index

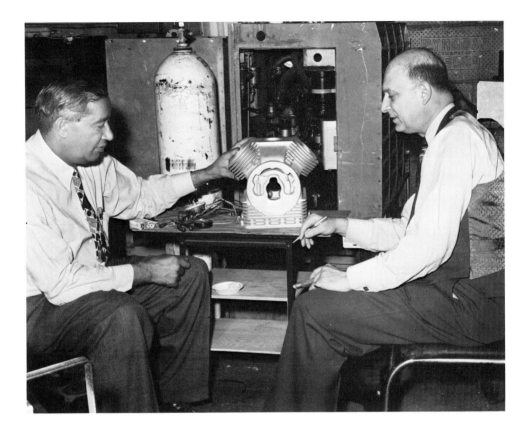

Photograph Acknowledgments

Thermo King: front cover, pp. 1, 2, 69, 76, 77, 80, 81, 93; Gloria Swanson: back cover, 27 (top), 40, 48, 53, 58, 67, 73, 75, 86, 91; Schomburg Center for Research in Black Culture, New York Public Library (original by Martin Luther King, Jr.): 7; Birmingham Public Library, Alabama: 8; Cincinnati Historical Society: 9, 13; Philadelphia Free Library, Automobile Reference Collection: 14; Missouri Historical Society: 19; Don H. Johnson: 22; Kittson County Historical Society: 26, 27 (bottom), 31, 34, 35, (original by Thermo King) 70, (original by *Saturday Evening Post*) 82, 83, 84; Minnesota Historical Society (original by A. H. Anderson): 28; Martha Wass, Hallock: 33; Virginia Ott: 38, 96; Museum of Modern Art, Film Stills Archives: 52; Minneapolis Public Library, Minneapolis Collection: 62.

Inside illustrations by Darren Erickson, © 1994 by Runestone Press. Background cover illustration by Brian Liedahl, © 1994 by Runestone Press.

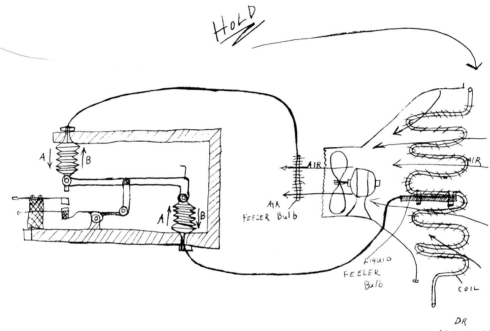

HOLD

A↓ ↑B

A↑ ↑B

AIR

AIR

AIR
FEELER Bulb

AIR

LIQUID
FEELER
Bulb

COIL

DR
MAY 12–42
AUTOMATIC DEFROSTING DEVICE

Drawn by Fred Jones